Glory in the Secret Place

Finding Intimacy with God

by

Bonnie Baldwin Briggs

DORRANCE
PUBLISHING CO
EST. 1920
PITTSBURGH, PENNSYLVANIA 15238

Dorrance Publishing Co
585 Alpha Drive
Pittsburgh, PA 15238
Visit our website at www.dorrancebookstore.com

ISBN: 979-8-88683-323-2
eISBN: 979-8-88683-716-2

Forward

In the following pages, my firm desire is that you be encouraged to go deeper into your walk with God. That you find a place of encouragement and spiritual depth that you have never experienced.

There are untold fathoms of new experiences with God through His Spirit that drive us to our knees in repentance and worship. To stand and shout the victory of His great power when you overcome adversity. To hear His gentle whisper in the night. As He reveals Himself through dreams and visions. These experiences are endless, yet I want to remind you to seek God and Jesus Christ first. That is the safest place to begin. Always put God first in your search for greater intimacy, not the experience.

You are a Spirit in a body. God is Spirit. Through your spirit, you will encounter the amazing visions, dreams, gifts, endowments of grace, and your ability to hear and see in the Spirit realm.

In your prayer closet, talk to the Lord and listen to Him. Take time and wait. There is an art to waiting on the Lord. It takes practice, but it is oh so worth it.

Start by picturing the stories in the Bible. Think about them and picture them in your mind. Read the verses that refer to dreams and visions to understand how God operates in the Spirit.

As we take this journey through this book together, stop often and apply some of the principles. Pray, and seek. He is waiting on you to hear Him!

Glory in the Secret Place

Finding Intimacy with God

Chapter 1

Spiritual Gifts

John 17: 18-21 (Amplified)

18: Just as You sent Me into the world, I also have sent them into the world.

19: And so, for their sakes and on their behalf, I sanctify (dedicate, consecrate, Myself, that they also may be sanctified (dedicated, consecrated, and made holy) by Truth; Your Word is Truth.

20: Neither for these alone do I pray (it is not for their sake only that I make this request), but also for all those who will ever come to believe in, trust in, cling to, rely on), Me through their word or teaching.

21: That they all may be one, (just) as You Father, are in Me and I in You, that they also may be one in Us so that the world may know and believe and be convinced that You have sent Me.

If you are reading this book, there is a hunger, yearning, and urgency in your heart to know God the Father as you have never known Him before. There is a deep yearning for a relationship with God that you have never experienced before. A drawing to intimacy that you know you need, but have never achieved.

My friend, read on, and let's explore the Spirit of God together.

The first revelation is not about you, but the Power of God working through you as you surrender to the Holy Spirit to operate in the Gifts of the Spirit.

I Corinthians 12: 1-11 (Amplified)

1: Now, about the spiritual gifts (the special endowments of supernatural energy), brethren, I do not want you to be misinformed.

2: You know that when you were heathen, you were led off after idols that could not speak (habitually) as impulse directed and whenever the occasion might arise.

3: Therefore, I want you to understand that no one speaking under the power and influence of the (Holy) Spirit of God can ever say, Jesus, be cursed! And no one can (really) say, Jesus is (my) Lord, except by and under the power and influence of the Holy Spirit.

4: Now, there are distinctive varieties and distributions of the endowments (gifts), extraordinary powers distinguishing certain Christians due to the power of Devine grace operating in their souls by the Holy Spirit, and they vary, but the (Holy) Spirit remains the same.

5: And there are distinctive varieties of service and ministrations, but it is the same Lord who is served.

6: And there are distinctive varieties of operation (of working to accomplish things), but it is the same God who inspires and energizes them all.

7: But to each one is given the manifestation of the (Holy) Spirit (the evidence, the spiritual illumination of the Spirit) for good and profit.

8: To one is given in and through the (Holy) Spirit (the power to speak) a message of wisdom and to another (the power to express) a word of knowledge and understanding according to the same (Holy) Spirit.

9: To another (wonderworking) faith by the same (Holy) Spirit, to another the extortionary powers of healing by the one Spirit.

10: To another the working of miracles, to another prophetic insight (the gift of interpreting the divine will and purpose), to another the ability to discern and distinguish between (utterances of true) spirits (and false ones), to other various kinds of (unknown) tongues, to another the ability to interpret (such) tongues.

11: All these (gifts, achievements, abilities) are inspired and brought to pass by one and the same (Holy) Spirit. Who apportions to each person individually (exactly) as He chooses?

All Christians can operate in one or the other gifts at any chosen time as the Holy Spirit chooses to use them. The gifts are not reserved for the leadership of the church. We are all called to function in the gifts and endowments of the Spirit.

As God's Covenant, people humble themselves and cry out to the Lord for a closer walk with hunger and yearning for our Savior; He will bring these endowments.

Apostle Paul said, "I would that ye all Prophesy." Seek the higher gifts of a revelatory nature. The very first thing is to seek the Kingdom of God and all His righteousness! Focus on Jesus and let Him lead you.

Empty yourself of all the fleshly things that might hinder you. Let the Holy Spirit fill you. Pray in tongues while you are doing your daily routine. Seek God as you have never sought Him before. Yield to Him; offer Him your entire being.

The Holy Spirit brings each gift into our lives as we need them or believe in them. When a child receives a gift from you, they are full of joy and excited to open and see what's inside. That is exactly how we should receive gifts from the Holy Spirit. It is a great adventure to operate in these gifts and see lives changed, church, family, community, and nations changed because you have been gifted by the Holy Spirit.

How exciting is that?

You are beginning or deepening your relationship with God that will bring many adventures in the Spirit as He leads you to people to speak into their lives. One of the greatest honors in a Child of God's life is to bring another to the saving knowledge of Jesus Christ. To set the captives free and deliver them from the power of the evil one, to heal the sick, and encourage those who are downcast. What an honor to be the mouth and hands of Jesus! So, stir up the Holy Spirit within you and move out bravely for the Lord.

One morning after an especially wonderful time with the Lord, I felt moved to declare some things into my life.

I went in front of a mirror and looked into my eyes and declared that I was a warrior woman for God, a prophetic Intercessor, a watchman on the wall. I declared I am strong, healthy, and vibrant by the power of the Lord flowing through me. That very morning, the Heavenly Father started speaking to me in a one-on-one conversation. I asked Him questions, and He answered them. There is a closeness that I have never experienced before.

This book is a direct result of that conversation.

God started directing me in daily prayer, where to pray to make my prayer more effective. Showing me where to aim the prayers in His will in different places around the country and world. To know that the Heavenly Father and Jesus are directly involved with your prayers is life changing. There is excitement to meet with the Lord daily and see what strongholds you will be part of destroying for that day. There is an awareness of His presence in and around you, His love, and His desire to be with you as you pray. You experience a new level of intimacy and adventure that is beyond explanation. Come with me as I share with you some of my adventures.

My friend, this intimacy is available to every Spirit-filled Believer. There are no favorites in God's Kingdom! Find a quiet place to close the door, quiet your mind and spirit, sit before the Lord, don't talk, just listen, expect to hear and receive. The Lord wants to talk to you. He craves this relationship with you! You will be more aware of His voice as you practice His presence.

John 10:27 (Amplified)

27. The sheep that are my own hear and are listening to my voice, and I know them, and they follow me.

Child of God, it is imperative you know and hear God's voice. He leads us where He wants us to go. His desires become our desires.

Psalms 37:4 (Amplified)

4. Delight yourself in the Lord, and He will give you the desires of your heart.

You see, when you delight yourself in the Lord, He changes your fleshly desires to His spiritual ones. You no longer want or crave the things of this world. You want and crave those things that honor and further the kingdom of God. Remember what I said at the beginning of this chapter.

This is all about God. His plans, His kingdom, His Spirit operating in and through us. His desires for us. We need to change our thinking and outlook. God wants us to live according to His plan. God does not conform to our plans for our lives. He wants us to conform to His plans for our lives!

Jerimiah 29:11 (Amplified)

11. I know the plans I have for you, declares the Lord, plans to prosper you and not harm you, plans to give you hope and a future.

This takes humility and sacrifice to walk in God's plans and not our own. God is looking for those that are humbly seeking Him, yearning, hungering, crying out for more of Him!

Here is an example of how God wants to change how we go about our everyday errands.

Years ago, I had the honor of helping my parents to doctor appointments and anything they needed. One morning, as I was getting ready to pick them up, the Lord told me to speak to the cardiologist. The Lord said, "Tell him that the decision He was making was the right one." I had no idea what that meant.

As we left the examining room, I told him what the Lord had spoken to me. He looked at me strangely and said, "I certainly hope you are right." Later I found out that he was moving his practice to another hospital. He needed that confirmation. How exciting to speak into another person's life about God's plans for them.

Challenge:

Practice sitting and listening for God to speak to you. Calm your mind and spirit. Write down whatever you hear. If there seems to be a hindrance, pray, and ask God to empty you of any negative thinking, unresolved sin, or unforgiveness that might hinder you from hearing from the Lord. Don't give up. Keep at it till you hear Him clearly. As we journey through these times of turmoil, it is so important that you hear from Jesus!

Declarations:

Stand before a mirror and make declarations about your life. Prophesy those things that are in the Spirit realm. Bring them into your life.

Example:

I am a warrior woman. I war against the powers of darkness that threaten my family, church, or community. I watch in the Spirit for directions the Lord wants me to see. I am strong and healthy, vibrant with the power of the Lord. I have the strength to accomplish the assignments the Lord has given me. God has given me discernment, wisdom, and knowledge for the times I live in.

Now declare whatever is relevant to your gifts and callings. Assert them into your life. Your words are full of power and build your faith.

Prayer:

Lord, I am so grateful for your presence in my life. I crave more time with you and an intimacy I have not experienced before. Lord, awaken my spirit. Help me to operate boldly and confidently in your gifts and callings on my life as together we change the lives of your treasured people. Open my ears to hear clearly and my eyes to see in the Spirit realm as your guide and direct me by your voice.

In Jesus' Name,

Amen

Chapter 2

Freedom From Fear and Failure

One hindrance to the free movement of the Holy Spirit through spiritual gifts and callings is FEAR! The fear of man must be overcome and moved past to move in the Holy Spirit with total freedom. God wants us to operate boldly and confidently through whatever we face.

When full of the Holy Spirit and power from on high, we can stand before world leaders and declare the truths of Heaven with the humble power of the Spirit without fear or dread.

Romans 12: 1-3 (Amplified)

I appeal to you, therefore, brethren, and beg of you in view of (all) the mercies of God, to make a decisive dedication of your bodies (presenting all your members and faculties) as a living sacrifice, holy (devoted, consecrated) and well-pleasing to God which is your reasonable service (rational, intelligent) service and spiritual worship.

Do not be conformed to this world (this age) (fashioned after and adapted to its external superficial customs) but be ye transformed (changed) by the (entire) renewal of your mind (by its new ideals and its new attitude), so that you may prove (for yourselves). What is good and acceptable and perfect for the will of God, even the thing which is good and acceptable and perfect (in His sight for you).

For by the grace (unmerited favor of God) given to me. I warn everyone among you not to think more highly than he ought (not to have an exaggerated opinion of his own importance) but to rate his ability with sober judgment each according to the degree apportioned him by God.

Paul cautioned us to dedicate ourselves. Sacrifice ourselves to the work of God and our relationship with Him, so we grow closer and more intimate daily. The above scripture is a mainstay of mine. It tells us that no matter what happens in our lives, family, church, or world, with a renewed mind and dedication to God, we can stand and face every battle with a firm-footed stance and win! We have all the knowledge and wisdom of God's Kingdom at our disposal if we will tap into it by renewing our minds.

By seeking to operate in the gifts and callings of the Holy Spirit, waking up every morning to a new adventure in prayer, relationships, prophetic encounters, lives changed and brought to our relationship with Jesus, there is no end to the spiritual adventures. With your mind renewed and transformed, each day holds a new understanding of God's perfect will for your life. With that comes the peace that passes understanding that you are where you need to be in God's perfect plan for your life!

I Corinthians 12:31 (Amplified)

31. But earnestly desire and zealously cultivate the great-

est and best gifts and graces (the highest and choicest graces). And yet I will show you a still more excellent way (one that is better by far and the highest of them all)—love.

We are to desire these spiritual gifts. Desire means to want, wish, long, crave, yearn. These are all strong words with the power to draw the Holy Spirit to us.

Zealously means fervent, fiery, passionate, enthusiastic, eager, wholehearted. These two words describe how we should pursue intimacy with God and spiritual gifts. Don't put anything ahead of your desire for God!

I Corinthians 14:1 (Amplified)

Eagerly pursue and seek to acquire (this) love (make it your aim, your great quest) and earnestly desire and cultivate the spiritual endowments (gifts, especially that you may prophesy, interpret the DeVine will in inspired preaching and teaching).

My friend, we need to passionately desire the gifts of the Holy Spirit. When you wake in the morning, it is on your heart to seek more and more of Jesus. Hunger and crave to hear His voice, to see Him in your dreams and visions. Because you are hungry for all God has for you.

What a glorious life and many adventures will be yours as you journey deeper into your relationship with God. There is no end, for He is eternal and fathomless. To see the people you react with changed for eternity. To go to your prayer room and know your prayers that day are changing history. To pray for healing and see that person healed. To have the King of kings and Lord of lords whisper in your ear the words and people to pray for and see situations changed for His Glory. What an adventure. There is great power in our words. God spoke this world in existence by His Word. Our words also have power. We can speak life or death using our words. Speak wisely.

When you start speaking God's truths over yourself and others, creative power flows forth, as much power as the day you were created in your mother's womb.

Psalms 71: 6-8 (Amplified)

6. Upon you have I leaned and relied from birth; You are He who took me from my mother's womb, and You have been my benefactor from that day. My praise is continual of You.

7. I am a wonder and a surprise to many. But You are my strong refuge.

8. My mouth shall be filled with Your praise and with Your honor all day.

My friend, from the day you were born, God has waited for you to be His voice on the earth. He wants you to be in an intimate relationship, Speak His words of truth, and change you, your family, community, and nations! With your voice powered by the Holy Spirit, the world will never be the same! Let's get started.

Declaration:

I am a warrior for God, the mighty King of the Universe. I speak with the creative power of the Holy Spirit. My thoughts are pure and full of love. I will pursue my Heavenly Father, His Son Jesus, and the Holy Spirit passionately so that I might walk pleasing to them.

Prayer:

I am looking to you, Heavenly Father, as we journey together Spirit to spirit. Open my spiritual eyes that I might see into the spirit realm. Open my spiritual ears to hear your softly spoken words. I love you, dear Lord.

In Jesus' Name,

Amen

Chapter 3

Overcoming Negative Self-Image

We now will approach the topic of self-image. I believe this is one of the greatest hindrances to flowing in the Holy Spirit because we have an image of ourselves that hinder us from receiving the Gifts of the Holy Spirit.

Let's see what God thinks of you.

John 3:16 (Amplified)

16. For God so greatly loved and dearly prized the world that He (even) gave up His only begotten (unique) Son so that whoever believes in Him (trusts in. clings to, relies on) shall not perish (come to destruction, be lost), but have eternal (everlasting) life.

Child of God, do you see how precious you are in God's sight. He gave His only Son for you to be saved! You are cherished and loved by God. You are a priceless gem. One who the Heavenly Father, Jesus, and the Holy Spirit want to partner with to help bring in this end-time harvest of souls. You were born for such a time as this!

Ephesians 1:3 (Amplified)

May blessings (praise, laudation, and eulogy) be to the God and our Father of our Lord Jesus Christ (the Messiah), Who has blessed in Christ with every spiritual (given by the Holy Spirit) blessing in the Heavenly realm.

You are so loved that God poured out every spiritual blessing from the Heavenly realm. My friend, start seeing yourself from God's eyes. Know who you are in Christ. Start speaking over yourself about who you are by the Word of God.

Example:

I am a child of God. My past is just that, my past. I will only remember it to show how far I have come. I am an overcomer. I have on the full armor of God and stand strong in the face of the enemy. I am on a quest to know the Lord in a deeper, more intimate way. Open my spiritual eyes so that I may see what you wish to show me, Lord. My home is a place of peace and refuge. I am loved and cherished by the Heavenly Father. I desire your presence and clearly hear you as you speak to my heart.

Here are some examples of the negative image in the Bible.

The Midianites were harassing Israel. Taking their crops and animals. Israel was hiding in caves and dens in the mountains. Israel was in a hard place. And cried out to the Lord for help.

Gideon was threshing grain hiding in a wine press. When he had a DeVine encounter.

Judges 6: 12-16 (Amplified)

12. And the Angel of the Lord appeared to him and said to him. The Lord is with you. You mighty man of (fearless) courage.

13. And Gideon said to him. O sir, if the Lord is with us, why is all this befallen us? Where are all His wondrous

works of which our fathers told us? Did not the Lord bring us up from Egypt? But now, the Lord has forsaken us and given us into the hands of the Midianites.

14. The Lord turned and said to him; Go in this your might, and you shall save Israel from the hand of the Midian.

15. Gideon said to Him; Oh Lord, how can I deliver Israel? Behold, my clan is the poorest in Manasseh, and I am the least in my father's house.

16. The Lord said to him, Surely, I will be with you, and you shall smite the Midianites as one man.

Do you see yourself as Gideon saw himself? Well, let's start to change that. Gideon's view of his father's clan was the most insignificant in Israel. He saw himself as the least in his father's house. Yet the Angel of the Lord said to him, the Lord is with you. You mighty man of courage. From that point on, the Lord worked with Gideon to change his self-image. God wants you to see yourself as a mighty man or woman of God that He has great plans for and great adventures to share as you minister together.

How do you see yourself?

I encourage you to stand before a mirror and declare that you are a mighty warrior for the Kingdom of God. Declare your prayers are changing history for your family, church, community, and nation! I am a major influence as a warrior for the Kingdom of God. I am humble, yet strong and mighty and full of grace!

As you grow in your positive self-image, you will have a greater prayer burden for those around you, your community, and the world events. You will have more confidence in your prayers because you know the Lord is there to partner with you, as you pray back the powers of darkness and shine your light into every situation you are praying for. God wants to use you to be His voice to a lost generation of His treasured people. To do that, you need to learn to hear and speak what God is saying. This takes practice, practice, practice.

Another example of poor self-image is in the book of Numbers. Moses sent out twelve spies into the promised land. Ten had an evil report when they returned, and two had a positive one.

Numbers 13: 32-33 (Amplified)

32. So, they brought the Israelites an evil report of the land which they had scouted out, saying; The land through which we went to spy it out is a land that devours its inhabitants, and all the people we saw in it were people of great stature.

33. There we saw Nephilim (or giants), the sons of Anak, who came from giants; we were in our own sight as grasshoppers, and so we were in their sight.

Numbers 14: 6-9 and 21-22 (Amplified)

6. And Joshua, son of Nun, and Caleb, son of Jephunneh, who were among the scouts who searched the land, rent their clothes.

7. And they said to all the company of the Israelites. The land to which we passed as scouts is an exceedingly good land.

8. If the Lord delights in us, then He will bring us into the land and give it to us. A land flowing with milk and honey.

9. Only do not rebel against the Lord, neither fear the people of the land, for they are bread for us. Their defense and shadow of (protection) is removed from over them. But the Lord is with us. Fear them not.

21. But truly, as I live, the earth shall be filled with the glory of the Lord.

God spoke to Moses about his anger at the Israelites.

22. Because all those men who have seen MY Glory and MY (miraculous) which I performed in Egypt and in the wilderness, yet have tested and proved Me these ten times and have not heeded My voice.

Did you catch the verse that says we were grasshoppers in our sight? That is a small self-image. God wanted them to see how powerful He was, and His protection is the important thing to believe. These men were still depending on their strength and not the Lord's.

When we see ourselves in our human weakness, we will not win many battles. But when we see ourselves as God sees us as powerful warriors in His sight. When we co-labor with the Lord and rely on His protection, strength, and miracle-working power, we now have a winning combination.

Do you see how important it is to see yourselves as God sees you in Christ? In Christ, we cannot be defeated. It is powerful to know how important the Lord is in your life. To know that the God of the Universe is with you every step you take, and victory is yours.

Declaration:

I am a warrior for the Kingdom of God. I am strong and bold for the Lord. Every day is a new adventure in the Spirit realm with my Jesus. In prayer and in my seeing into the Spirit realm. I lay my life before you and humbly use those gifts You have given me.

Prayer:

Lord, reveal yourself to me. I want to hear your voice. I want to grow into new areas of the Prophetic. I desire all

Your gifts and to speak Your words as You speak to me.
That I may win souls for Your Kingdom and Your Glory.
In Jesus' Name,
Amen

Chapter 4

Moving Forward

I want to ask you a question. Are you on the move, or are you waiting for God to move you?

God is looking for people who know who they are in Christ Jesus to boldly move forward into the call of God on their lives. People who fear and reverence Him. Brave warriors who, through the power of the Holy Spirit working in them, pray in the Holy Spirit to battle the enemies of God! The following scriptures give us insight into how to do warfare and be moving in the Holy Spirit with great effectiveness. It is a long scripture; however, it is powerful for our daily walk!

Ephesians 6:10-18 (Amplified)

10. In conclusion, be strong in the Lord (be empowered through your union with Him); draw your strength from Him. (That strength which His boundless might provides).

11. Put on God's whole armor (the armor of a heavy-armed soldier which God supplies) that you may be able

successfully to stand up against (all the strategies and deceits of the devil)

12. For we are not wrestling with flesh and blood (contending only with physical opponents), but against (the master spirits who are) the world rulers of this present darkness, against the spirit forces of wickedness in the heavenly (supernatural) sphere.

13. Therefore, put on God's complete armor so that you may be able to resist and stand your ground on the evil day (of danger) and have done all (the crisis demands) to stand (firmly in your place).

14. Stand, therefore (hold your ground), having tightened the belt of truth around your loins and having put on the breastplate of integrity and moral rectitude and right standing with God.

15. And having shod your feet with the preparation (to face the enemy with firm footed stability, the promptness, and the readiness, produced by the Good News), of the Gospel of Peace.

16. Lifting up, over all the (covering) shield of saving faith, upon which you can quench all the flaming missals of the wicked one.

17. And take the helmet of salvation and the sword that the Spirit wields, which is the Word of God.

18. Pray at all times (on every occasion, in every season) in the Spirit with all (manner of prayer and entreaty. To that end, keep alert and watch with strong purpose and perseverance interceding on behalf of all saints (God's consecrated people).

The above scriptures are a direction from the Apostle Paul to be always prepared by making sure we are covered in our spiritual armor. Notice the scriptures say to PUT on armor. It is not automatic, because you received Jesus Christ as your Savior. We, as Christians, need to be always prepared with our armor in place. When we recognize who our enemies really are, it gives us a great advantage over the devil. Satan and his minions like to hide behind flesh and blood (people), so you won't call him out and declare victory over him. You have the authority over him, Child of God.

In verse thirteen, it says to make sure your armor is in place to resist the devil, and stand your ground on the evil day of danger. It does not say God will block the danger. It says you will resist and stand in the face of danger. Using the truth of God's Word and your right standing with God, you can face down any demon from Hell with the armor of God in place.

Why? Because you prepared ahead of time for the battle. You are preparing when you read God's Word. Pray, you will have a firm foundation to stand on to do supernatural battle with the enemy, using your faith in God as a shield against any enemy's attack. Always Pray in the Spirit (tongues) to keep watch, be alert, be purposeful, praying for God's covenant people.

Do you notice in Ephesians 6:10-18 that it is action on our parts, put on, stand firmly, resist, read the Word of God, and apply faith? It is action moving in the Spirit of God! Moving forward in the plans God has for you.

Matthew 6:33 (Amplified)

But seek (aim at and strive after), first of all, His Kingdom and His righteousness (His way of doing and being right). And then all these things taken together will be given you besides.

The whole Kingdom of God is action, loving, forgiving, prayer, long-suffering, joy, kindness, humility, self-control, and on and on requires action on our part. It is a choice and a move of your free will to practice all these actions as a child of God.

The Lord wants us to set our minds, thoughts, and actions on heavenly things.

Colossians 3:1-2 (Amplified)

If you have been raised with Christ (to a new life, thus sharing His resurrection from the dead), aim at and seek the (rich, eternal treasures) that are above, where Christ is seated at the right hand of the God.

And set your minds and keep them set on what is above (the higher things), not the things on this earth.

When you press into seeking God and His righteousness, you will become aware of things in your life that are not sins, but do not bring honor and glory to God.

I love to read. My favorite genre, other than Christian books, is historical western fiction. I had never been convicted by my reading. The Lord convicted me of how much time I spent reading western novels, and He would prefer I use that time setting my mind on Him. The Lord was asking me to make a sacrifice to step into a greater level of intimacy with Him. I made the decision and now only read what glorifies God, lifts my spirit, and encourages me in my walk with the Lord.

During this time, I remember a story about Smith Wigglesworth. He would not even allow a newspaper to be brought into his home. He valued the anointing of the Lord so much he would not allow worldly commentary in his home. Smith Wigglesworth did great miracles and works for the Lord.

I crave a deeper and closer relationship with the Lord. That is more important than reading a novel!

Declaration:

I set my mind on things above where Jesus sets at the right hand of the Father. I will only read or watch those things that bring honor and glory to God. I will meditate on the Bible stories to familiarize myself more deeply with God's Word.

Prayer:

Lord, I love you, and thank you for your presence. I honor and reverence you. Today, Lord, may every thought, word, or deed I accomplish please You and the Heavenly Father. May I further the Kingdom of God through my thoughts, actions, and words.

In Jesus' Name,

Amen

Chapter 5

Make The Most of Your Time.

The days we are living in are challenging, to say the least. The Lord chooses us to be born at such a time as this. We are His end-day warriors. We see the ever-present darkness trying to rob us of our freedom, peace, religious liberty, and happiness. However, when we keep our spiritual eyes open to God's presence and power working in our lives through intimacy with the Lord. We get a different view. The Lord wants us to live purposefully. Look at the following scriptures that show us to redeem the time to make every minute count for the Kingdom of God.

Ephesians 5: 14-17 (Amplified)

14. Therefore, He says, Awake oh sleeper, and arise from the dead and Christ shall shine (make day dawn) upon you and give you light.

15. Look carefully then how you will walk. Live purposefully and worthily and accurately not as the unwise and witless, but as wise (sensible, intelligent people).

16. Making the very most of your time (buying up each opportunity) because the days are evil.

17. Therefore, do not be vague and thoughtless and foolish, but understanding and firmly grasp what the will of the Lord is.

To live a life of purpose and in the will of the Lord takes thought, renewing your mind to God's will, not the world's way of thinking. Learn to pace yourself in God's timing and will for the day. You may feel a call in your life. That is a wonderful thing. However, make sure the timing is right. We must not get ahead of God's timing.

The story of David's life is a powerful example of God's timing and respect for authority working in David's life. He was first anointed to be King at the age of fifteen. He was anointed the second time to be King over Judah at thirty. David spent a lot of time waiting on God's timing. He had tremendous respect for authority. He was a man of a humble and repentant heart.

See, I Samuel 16: 12-13 and II Samuel 5: 6

The importance of timing in God's Kingdom cannot be overstated. That does not mean we are not being active in God's plan; it just means we might have some growing and maturing to do before we are ready for the full authority of God's calling.

When we are operating in the realm of the Holy Spirit, we need to be aware of what the Lord is doing. He is omnipresent, so His presence is multifaceted. He can be working to answer your prayers while working in another realm at the same time! Mind-blowing, isn't it? That's why timing is so important in God's work.

When we make the most of our time, it is important to not get bogged down and not enjoy the simple things in life, family, friends, and relationships that will help us grow. I enjoy my secret time with Jesus so much that I must remind myself to breathe. Make time to fellowship with a good meal around the table and catch up with those who mean the most to us. It is good medicine!

With so much going on, we sometimes forget that our human minds are very time orientated. However, God lives in the eternal realm. He does not live in minutes, hours, days, and years. He is in eternity, so reign in your impatient thoughts and let God's peace flow through you. God is always on time!

While you are waiting on God's time, study God's Word, pray, and seek His way and presence. Remember that being idle is a waste of time, and God wants you to seek Him. Ask for new revelations, wisdom, knowledge, and discernment to be revealed to you as you wait on the Lord. Press, pursue, into the Lord, so you will know God's perfect timing in all things. Use your time wisely. Because the days are evil, so we must be focused on pushing back against the enemy in prayer for our family, church, community, and nation.

Habakkuk 2:3 (Amplified)

For the vision is yet for an appointed time, and it hastens to the end (fulfillment), it will not deceive or disappoint. Though it tarry wait (earnestly) for it; because it will surely come; it will not be behindhand on its appointed day.

Proverbs 3: 5-6 (Amplified) 5. Lean on, trust in, and be confident in the Lord with all your heart and mind and do not rely on your own insight or understanding.

6. In all your ways, know, recognize, and acknowledge Him, and He will direct and make straight and plain your paths.

When you live a life of making the most of your time, you purposely mark your day by prayer, God's Word, and operating in your giftings. There is a purpose for God's Kingdom in all you do. Know you are in God's perfect will.

Romans 12:1-2 (Amplified)

I appeal to you therefore, brethren and beg of you in view of (all) the mercies of God, to make a decisive dedication of your bodies (presenting all your members and faculties) as a living sacrifice, holy (devoted, consecrated) and well pleasing to God, which is your reasonable (rational, intelligent), service and spiritual worship.

Do not be conformed to this world (this age, fashioned after and adapted to its external superficial customs) but be ye transformed (changed) by the (entire) renewal of your mind (by its new ideals and its new attitude so that you may prove (for yourselves) what is the good and acceptable and perfect will of God for You (In His sight for you).

These verses are a light into the way of entering into an intimacy with the Lord. The Apostle Paul says we cannot know the will of God without a renewed mind, a transformed mind. When your mind is transformed and renewed, you no longer look at the world or your life the same way. You have new Ideals (God's Ideals). Your attitude becomes God's attitude. You strive to please Him in all you say and do.

In the above scriptures, it says do not be conformed.

Conformed: To be like someone or something.

Transformed: To change the condition or purpose of someone or thing.

As we look at the definition of these words, we see why the author used them. Don't be conformed to this world, but be ye transformed to God's image, desires, and mind-set. Then and only then can you know the perfect will of God for your life.

In this chapter on making the most of your time, every mundane chore and task can bring glory and honor to the Lord. When shopping, look for an opportunity to speak into the stock person or cashier's life. Put your grocery cart back to make the cart boy's job easier. Ask how the person in the drive-thru food place is doing, and wish them a good day.

This is a lifestyle of purpose, making the most of your time in all you do, for the days are evil, shine your light.

Colossians 3:16-17 (Amplified)

16. Let the Word (spoken by) Christ (the Messiah) have its home (in your hearts and minds) and dwell in you in (all its) richness, as you teach and admonish and train one another in all insight and intelligence and wisdom (in Spiritual things and as you sing), Psalms, Hymns, and Spiritual songs, making melody to God, with His grace in your hearts.

17. And whatsoever you do (no matter what it is) in word, deed, do everything, in the name of the Lord Jesus and in (dependence upon) His person and giving praise to God the Father through Him.

Reading these scriptures is eye-opening to us to show how important all we do has meaning and purpose. We are admonished to do everything as unto the Lord. Our lives take on a whole new dimension and excitement, a sense of adventure, because you are working for the Lord in all the mundane tasks that may be under-appreciated by those around you. But when you are doing that task for Jesus, that changes everything. Why because every task takes on a new perspective of blessing and honoring the King! Now that's redeeming your time!

Declaration:

I am a warrior for the Lord. I honor Father God, Jesus Christ, and the Holy Spirit in everyday tasks. I am a warrior serving my Lord with honor and grace. Today we will accomplish great work together. Many battles will be won as I go through my day.

Prayer:

Thank you, Lord, for another day. Today I praise and honor you, and pray you will fill the person reading this book with bold urgency to redeem the day, for evil is abounding. However, You are greater than any evil. You can face any darkness of this present time. Pour out Your Spirit on the Lord and open the eyes to see that their time spent in Your presence is life changing.

In Jesus' Name,

Amen

Chapter 6

The Power of Your Words

As the Church of Jesus Christ, The Body of Christ, we have a mighty power in our words. Too often, we take this lightly. Our words hold life and death. There is power in our words to create and build the life you know God is anointing you to build, to build up other people. To create or tear down. Look at the following scripture to see what I mean.

Proverbs 18: 20-21 (Amplified)

20. A man's (moral) self shall be filled with the fruit of his mouth and the consequence of his words. He must be satisfied (whether good or evil).

21. Death and life are in the power of the tongue, and they who indulge in it shall eat the fruit of it (for either life or death).

We should soberly consider our words before we speak. For we have been given the power of life and death, blessing and cursing in our words. That is a powerful statement.

I want my words to bring created life to the person who hears and receives them. Do you want to create a life of peace, love, and grace? Through our words and relationship through Jesus to our Heavenly Father, it is possible.

Matthew 12: 35-37 (Amplified)

35. The good man from his good inner treasure flings forth good things, and the evil man out of his inner evil storehouse flings forth evil things.

36. But I tell you, on the day of judgment, men will have to give an account for every idle (inoperative, non-working) word they speak.

37. For by your words, you will be justified and acquitted, and by your words, you will be condemned and sentenced.

You see, our words determine what is in our hearts. Do your words bring encouragement, life, build up, or tear down?

Right now, search your heart. If you are convicted of words you spoke, repent and ask forgiveness from the person you spoke to. Ask the Lord to forgive you. Then determine in your heart with the help of the Lord to guard your tongue in the future. This may take some time to accomplish if you have a habit of speaking your mind. Be patient and follow God's lead, and you will overcome.

Since we are created in God's image, God spoke this world into existence by His Word. We have creative power in our words by faith. Jesus said, "If you have the faith the size of a mustard seed, you can say to this mountain be thou removed, and that mountain moves!" We should cherish this ability and grow in it. The deeper and more mature your faith and belief in God's Word through us, the more powerful our walk with Jesus. This is part of living a life of purpose in Christ.

As you realize, every word you speak has a purpose and creative power. Then you will not allow idle words to flow from you and defile the flow of the Holy Spirit in your life. Great things are in store for you, my friend. Your words start creating new precious things in your life that were absent before. Our words form a testimony of who we are and what we believe. Full of faith, believing for those things that are not as though they were, they may not be visible in the natural ream but by our words and faith combined bringing those things that are not seen in the natural from the Spirit realm to the natural realm. That's the creative power of words combined with faith.

Hebrews 11: 1-3 (Amplified)

Now faith is the assurance (the confirmation, the title deed) of the things (we) hope for, being the proof of things (we) do not see and the conviction of their reality (faith perceiving as real fact, what is not revealed to the senses.

For by faith (trust and holy fervor born of faith), the men of old had a divine testimony born to them and obtained a good report.

By faith, we understand that the worlds (during successive ages) were framed (fashioned, put in order, and equipped for their intended purpose) by the Word of God so that what we see was not made from the things which are visible.

Wow.

What a privilege we have in Jesus Christ's body to speak those things that are not as though they were. What do you want to see manifest in your life? Write them down, date them, and start speaking those things. I am not talking about worldly things. I am talking about Spiritual endowments. Then start speaking them into your life.

Our words can change the spiritual atmosphere in our minds, room, church service, community, and nation. That is how powerful our words are. When you blend your faith with your words, powerful things happen for God's glory.

Matthew 6:33 (Amplified)

33. But seek ye first the Kingdom of God and His righteousness, and all these things shall be added unto you.

The order of believing for and speaking into existence those things that are not as though they had an order. First and foremost, we need to seek the Kingdom of God. Seek Him and His righteousness. Seek God while He may be found. Praise and worship Him for His honor and glory. Make God first in your Life!

Then press in by faith and belief for all the things you desire to manifest in your life. The wisdom of God, revelation in the spirit realm, visions, dreams, hearing God in your heart, and operating in the Spirit's gifts. What an exciting journey we are on. What an honor to partner with our Heavenly Father, Jesus Christ, and the Holy Spirit to bring creative wonders and miracles, healing, finances, children, and more into being by faith and the power of our words.

Declaration:

I declare that I will make the best use of my time to honor, glorify, and further the Kingdom of God. I will use my words to build, strengthen, and create positive relationships. I will speak life and not death.

Prayer:

Lord, I praise and honor you! Great is the Lord and greatly to be praised. I want to see you, Jesus. I want more of you. I hunger for your presence hour by hour. I long for your touch. Reveal Yourself to me so that I may have a vision in my heart and spirit. Oh Lord, I love spending my time with you. You are my strength and refuge.

In Jesus' Name,

Amen

Chapter 7

Journey In the Supernatural

Early in my Christian journey, my family lived in Montana at the time. I had my four daughters in our van, and we drove out in the country to look at some property we were interested in. After looking at it, we all got back in the van. I turned the key, and nothing, just a click. My heart sank as I realized we were out in the middle of nowhere, and the battery was dead.

As I sat there pondering what to do, I turned to the girls and said we needed to pray for the van to start. Being innocent children, they were very excited to pray for something practical as starting our van. We prayed for the Lord to send us help or fix the van. Glory be to God, He did!

One of the children pointed to a man walking across the field in the middle of nowhere. At first, I was concerned because we were so isolated. The gentleman was large, tall, and muscular. He wore bib overalls and work boots. He was very polite when he asked what was wrong.

I told him about the ignition problem. He told me to put the van in neutral, and he would push it.

Well, even I knew you needed to reach a greater speed than a man could manage to start the van. However, the van started, and when I turned to thank him, he was gone. The children were just as stunned as I was to realize we had just had an angelic visitation! This story opens a look into the supernatural in our natural world.

The precious Heavenly Father, through Jesus' name, heard our cries and sent a Heavenly messenger (angel) to help my little girls and me safely home. He hears and moves on the fervent prayer of hearts believing Him for help.

When we start seeking, searching, and crying out for more of Jesus Christ, a deeper understanding of His ways, we open our lives to exciting moves of the Holy Spirit as He reveals Jesus and the Spirit realm to us.

The Holy Spirit is our teacher and opens understanding we may not have in our natural minds. But the Holy Spirit can reveal those things to us. Opening our eyes, ears, and hearts more of the heart of God through your spirit. God is a Spirit. You are a spirit in a body. So how you communicate with Lord is His Spirit to your spirit. God desires to connect with you intimately as you commune with Him in your prayer closet or quiet place of prayer, waiting on Him in that secret place. His Spirit joined with yours, so you can flow freely your communion with Him.

God is no respecter of persons. If He will send an angel to a lady and her children in the middle of nowhere, He will certainly send them on assignment to anyone.

Now a word of caution, we are to worship God, Jesus Christ, and the Holy Spirit. Angels are not to be worshiped.

They are messengers sent by God to the children of God or whatever assignment the Heavenly Father sends them on. We do not command angels or ask for them to do anything. They are God's messengers for Him alone to command. Always seeking the Kingdom of God and His righteousness, and all these things will be added to you.

Matthew 6:33 (Amplified)

33. But seek (aim at and strive after) first of all His kingdom and His righteousness (His way of doing and being right), and then all these things taken together will be given to you besides.

All those things talked about in this scripture are addressed in earlier verses. Clothing, food, drink, and all the everyday things we need to sustain life. We need to seek Him first, then He will reveal a way to have those things. Hard work and applying yourself will be the most likely way.

Acts 1:5 and 8-11 (Amplified)

5. But John baptized with water, but not many days from now you shall be baptized with (placed in, introduced into) the Holy Spirit.

On the day Jesus ascended into Heaven, Jesus was teaching how important it is to be baptized in the Holy Spirit. Why? Because it is the power to operate in the anointing of God, in all you do for the Lord. Through the Holy Spirit, you can discern the wisdom, knowledge, and Spirit realm activity around you. It is so necessary to your walk in the Lord.

8. But you shall receive power (ability, efficiency, and might) when the Holy Spirit has come upon you. You shall be my witnesses in Jerusalem, and all Judea, and Samaria, and to the ends (the very bounds) of the earth.

9. And when He had said this, even as they were looking (at him), He was caught up, and a cloud carried Him away out of their sight.

10. And while they were gazing intently into the heaven as He went, behold two men (dressed) in white robes suddenly stood beside them.

11. Who said, men of Galilee, why do you stand here gazing into heaven? This same Jesus, who was caught away and lifted up from among you into heaven, will return (just) the same way in which you saw Him go into heaven!

Acts 1:5 gives a clear picture of Jesus explaining the Baptism of the Holy Spirit. The twelve disciples that were with Him during His ministry already believed He was the Son of God. However, they lacked in the Baptism of the Holy Spirit to do wonders, miracles carrying the anointing to heal the sick, raise the dead, and lead untold thousands to Jesus. The baptism of the Holy Spirit was needed then and is needed today.

Matthew 6:33 extorts us to seek God, and His righteousness and ALL these things shall be added unto you. Our Heavenly Father loves to give us good things. The Gifts of the Holy Spirit are part of those endowments, along with the fruit of the Spirit, those things we need to properly use in our daily lives. God desires to give us good gifts and endowments. SEEK HIM!

I left speaking in tongues for last because it is the only one of the Spiritual Gifts that build us as Christians in our own Spirits. That is why the enemy of our souls fights so hard against this gift. He knows as we pray in tongues that our spirit is getting stronger. Satan cannot understand the words of tongues we speak, so it is our secret language to pray to the Father God without Satan setting an ambush for us.

I Corinthians 14:4 (Amplified)

He who speaks in a (strange) tongue edifies and improves himself, but he who prophesies (interpreting the divine will and purpose and teaching with inspiration) edifies and improves the church and promotes growth (in Christian wisdom, piety, holiness, and happiness.

We need this gift or endowment of speaking in tongues to keep us uplifted as individuals, to improve and grow in our personal lives.

We need it to help others desire this gift so they may grow into mature Christians. To be uplifted in their most Holy faith.

What an incredible honor to co-labor with Jesus through the Holy Spirit, to flow and prepare you for whatever might happen that day or weeks ahead. You will be ready for it. Why? Because the Holy Spirit will prepare you, if you are listening.

In Chapter Four, we outlined putting on the armor of God. Read those verses again in preparation for any obstacle or hindrance in your way. Recognize that we do not wrestle with flesh and blood but evil spirits that can only be defeated in the spirit realm. You cannot fight evil spirits in your natural mind or strength. It must be through your spirit and the Word of God.

When you focus on Jesus, be strong in Him, empowered by Him. Stand strong, not in your strength but in the strength of Jesus. All your weapons and protection come from Jesus and the Holy Spirit. We have all our authority to take on Spiritual Warfare before and through Jesus.

Declaration:

I am strong through my relationship with Jesus. I stand firm footed because of the truth of God's Word, righteous in integrity, and right standing with God. My faith in Jesus will shield me from the fiery darts of the wicked one. I am an overcomer through Jesus.

Prayer:

Thank you, Lord, for giving me the tools and weapons to stand strong against any enemy attack. Thank you that I am not alone at any time. Through You, Lord, I commit my whole being. I bring myself into submission to your will.

In Jesus' Name,

Amen

Chapter 8

Preparing to do Spiritual Warfare

Spiritual warfare looks much different than warfare in the natural world. It is a warfare of the spirit realm. When need to learn to discern the spirits to be able to war against them. These evil spirits will attack our loved ones, family, and friends. And it is imperative that you know how to use your weapons and the Word of God to fight and tear down strongholds. Because Satan and his demons appear as messengers of light. That makes it important to know and discern the difference between God's messengers and the messengers of the evil realm.

The following scripture describes more about spiritual warfare.

II Corinthians 10:3-7 (Amplified)

For though we walk (live) in the flesh, we are not carrying on our warfare according to the flesh and using mere human weapons.

For the weapons of our warfare are not physical (weapons of flesh and blood), but they are mighty before God for the overthrow and destruction of strongholds.

(In as much as we) refute arguments and theories and reasonings and every proud and lofty thing that sets itself the true knowledge of God, and we lead every thought and purpose away captive into the obedience of Christ (the Messiah, the Anointed One).

Being in readiness to punish every (insubordinate for his) disobedience when your own submission and obedience (as a church) are fully secured and complete.

Look at (this obvious fact) which is before your eyes. If anyone is confident that he is Christ's, let him reflect and remind himself that even as he is in Christ, so are we. This scripture makes it plain that our weapons are of the Holy Spirit through and by Jesus Christ. The weapons are many, but I will list some of them to help you with your moving into being a warrior!

Praise:

Satan and his demons hate it when we praise God. Praise can release the presence of God in a way no other action can. When we praise the enemy cannot speak accusations or try to destroy our confidence. When you praise, you focus on our redeemer, which is warfare of the truest kind.

Blood of Jesus:

When praying and engaging in spiritual warfare, applying the blood of Jesus to a person or situation can defeat the enemy's assignment on that person or situation. Even Satan cannot cross the bloodline.

Word of God:

In Luke, we see the way Jesus used the Word of God to

defeat the devil. We can apply this as our example of how to war in the spirit.

Luke 4: 1-14 (Amplified)

The full of and controlled by the Holy Spirit returned from Jordan and was led (by) the (Holy) Spirit.

For (during) forty days in the wilderness (desert) where He was tempted (tried, tested, exceedingly) by the devil. He ate nothing during those days, and when they were completed, He was hungry.

The devil said to Him, If You are the Son of God, order these stones to turn into a loaf (of bread).

And Jesus replied to him, it is written, man shall not live and be sustained by (on) bread alone but by every word and expression of God.

Then the devil took Him up to a high mountain and showed Him all the kingdoms of the habitable world in a moment of time (in the twinkling of an eye).

And he said to Him, to you I will give all this power and authority and their glory (all their magnificent, excellence, preeminence, dignity and grace), for it has been turned over to me, I will give it to whomever I will.

Therefore,

If You will do homage to and worship me (just once), it shall all be Yours.

And Jesus replied to him, get thee behind Me, Satan! It is written. You shall do homage to and worship the Lord your God, and He only shall you serve.

Then he took Him to Jerusalem and set Him on the gable of the temple, and said to Him, if You are the Son of God, cast Yourself down from here.

For it is written, He will give His angel charge to watch over you to guard and watch over You closely and carefully.

And on their hands, they will bear You up, lest You strike your foot against a stone.

And Jesus replied to him, (the scripture) says you shall not tempt (try, test, exceedingly) the Lord your God.

And when the devil had ended every (the complete cycle of) temptation, he (temporarily) left Him (that is stood off from Him) until another more opportune and favorable time).

Then Jesus went back full of and under the control of the (Holy) Spirit into Galilee, and the fame of Him spread through the whole region roundabout.

Just as Jesus used the Word of God, so should we in every temptation of the enemy, fleshly struggle, praying for our family, friends, and church. The devil must back off and let you alone because you resisted him with the Word of God. He will wait in the shadows for another time, hoping to catch you off guard. So don't let your guard down.

Prayer:

Prayer is not only to prepare you for warfare. It is warfare. Pray without ceasing, pushing back on all the plans of the enemy.

Your testimony:

This is a key to a successful walk in the Lord. We remember our testimony. And share it often, how you came to the Lord is so powerful, and the enemy hates when you show how powerful Jesus' blood is to forgive every sin.

Revelation 12:11 (Amplified)

And they overcame (conquered) him by means of the blood of the Lamb and by the utterance of their testimony, for they did not love and cling to life even when faced with death (holding their lives cheap till they had to die for their witnessing).

Your testimony is a powerful weapon against the devil and his demon host. Use it and apply the blood of Jesus in every battle you can. The devil cannot cross the bloodline.

Gifts of the Holy Spirit:

We discussed this in an earlier chapter, so I ask you to refer to the chapter on Spiritual Gifts if you need to refresh your memory. For example, you can use the discerning of spirits to discern what evil spirit you might be in warfare against. Word of wisdom or knowledge will often give you the name of the spirit. So, you can cast down that stronghold. Scripture tells us to desire the best gifts.

These are just some spiritual weapons that will help you stand firm and strong when the enemy is harassing you. Remember, he only has the power you give him. If you stand strong in God's Word, you will win.

Humility:

This may sound like a strange weapon. However, the Lord Jesus remained humble through all His temptations, trials, and even death. Why? Because He knew that all His power was not in Him. It was from the Heavenly Father. So, with us, our authority and power come from the Heavenly Father, through Jesus and the Holy Spirit. We are nothing without them. Remember that, and you will stay humble in all the temptation to be puffed up because God is using you.

Fasting: When we fast food, there is a sacrifice on our part. When we focus our spiritual eyes on the Lord, there is a clarity that takes place in our spirits to bring strength and power from God to our prayers.

Declaration:

As a warrior in the Holy Spirit, I declare that through the name and blood of Jesus, I have authority over the devil and his unholy host. As I use the Word of God and my weapon and sword. Every demon must flee and leave as I pray and defeat the strongholds in my family, friends, church, community, and nation. While praising my Lord and Savior through every battle. Using my testimony to prove God's power in a person's life.

Prayer:

Heavenly Father, as we labor together to defeat the enemy. Letting our light shine and our salt flavor our world. I praise your name and know all authority and power come through the name and blood of Jesus. Protect the dear one reading this book. Cover them with your all-compassing protection as they join us in spiritual warfare. Direct them and guide them.

In Jesus' Name,

Amen

Chapter 9

Knowing Who You Are in Christ

As a Christian who has been born again by believing in and through the blood of Jesus, a truly remarkable thing happens. Before being born again, we saw ourselves as flesh and blood human beings. However, after being born again, we are a new creation, a spirit in a body. Because of this change, we can now commune Spirit to spirit with the Heavenly Father and Jesus in a new fulling way.

Ephesians 1: 3-14 (Amplified)

May blessing (praise, laudation, and eulogy) be to the God and Father of our Lord Jesus Christ (The Messiah), Who has blessed us in Christ with every spiritual (given by the Holy Spirit) blessing in the heavenly realm.

Even as (in His great love) He chose us (actually picked us out for Himself as His own) in Christ before the foundation of the world, that we should be holy (consecrated and set apart for Him) and blameless in His sight, even above reproach, before Him in love.

For He foreordained us (destined us, planned in love for us) to be adopted (revealed) as His own children through Jesus Christ, in accordance with the purpose of His will (because it pleased Him and was His own kind intent).

(So that we might be) to the praise and commendation of His glorious grace (favor and mercy), which He so freely bestowed on us in the Beloved.

In Him, we have redemption (deliverance and salvation) through His blood. The remission (forgiveness of our offenses and shortcomings and trespasses) in accordance with the riches and generosity of His gracious favor.

Which He lavished upon us in every kind of wisdom and understanding (practical insight and prudence).

Making known to us the mystery (secret) of His will (of His plan, purpose). (And it is this.) In accordance with His good pleasure (His merciful intention), which He had previously purposed and set for in Him.

(He planned) for the maturity of the times and the climax of the ages to unify all things and head them up and consummate them in Christ, (both) things in heaven and things on earth.

In Him, we also were made (God's) heritage (portion), and we obtain an inheritance, for we had been foreordained (chosen and appointed beforehand) in accordance with His purpose. Who works out everything in agreement with the counsel and design of His (own) will.

So that we who first hoped in Christ (who first put our confidence in Him have been destined and appointed to) live for the praise of His glory.

In Him, you also who have heard the Word of Truth, the glad tidings (Gospel) of your salvation and have believed in and adhered to and relied on Him, were stamped with the seal of the long-promised Holy Spirit.

That (Spirit) is the guarantee of our inheritance (first fruits, the pledge, the foretaste, the down payment on your heritage) in anticipation of its full redemption and our acquiring (complete possession of it to the praise of His glory.

The complete understanding of these scriptures to years of study for me to understand my position in Christ. The complete work that Christ did on that day on Calvary. The wholeness of or oneness in Christ. We have such an attachment to these mortal bodies that grasping what the Apostle Paul was saying took a lot of maturing and prayer on my part to understand. When we truly grasp this truth of who we are in Christ, it will change our world. In Him, we live!

Acts 17:28 (Amplified)

28. For in Him, we live and move and have our being, as even some of your (own) poets have said. For we are also His offspring.

When we know who we are in Christ, we will live in Jesus, speak in Jesus, pray in Jesus, warfare in Jesus, all for His glory and honor. Our lives will reflect His love and peace.

You are a spirit in a body of flesh. God is a Spirit. We must learn to separate our fleshly emotions and worldly thoughts from our spirit man. Feed your spirit man often, the Word of God, Godly books, sermons, feed your spirit as much or more than your fleshly body. Set aside time every day to focus on Jesus and meditate on God's Word and the visions, dreams, and miracles in God's word.

You will never be the same, your whole perspective changes. You are no longer living for Yourself. You seek Him for every decision, include Him in your daily activities, your fellowship with Him, and crave more time to spend with Him. Ask Him to help you pray and share words of comfort with those around you. This is the way we co-labor with the Lord. Expect Him to interrupt you and send you on spiritual adventures.

Declaration:

Today in Christ, there is victory in every battle as we war in Christ. I am assured of victory because He is the authority of all. Jesus in me, and I in Him, is a winning combination. I will fight with my full armor in my prayer closet, with wisdom, revelation, and power that Jesus has given to me!

Prayer:

Thank you, Lord, for a day of peace, love, revelation, and wisdom as I walk in you. We become one in our overcoming power through the Holy Spirit. I ask you to give me insight into the Holy Spirit so that I may see more clearly. You have blessed me with every spiritual blessing in the Heavenly realm. Lord, my desire is to walk pleasing in your sight and will today.

In Jesus' Name,

Amen

Chapter 10

Meeting in the Secret Place

There is a secret place prepared for each of us to meet with the Lord. It is there that we meet with Jesus and our Heavenly Father. I have met with Jesus alone at different times. Each time was personal and refreshing. As you focus on Jesus and journey further into intimacy with the Lord, the easier it becomes to hear and see into the spirit realm.

I have a room in my house where I can shut the door for privacy and quiet as I focus on Jesus and His plans for that day.

Matthew 6:6 (Amplified)

6. But when you pray, go into your (most) private room and, closing the door, pray to your Father who is in secret, and your Father who sees in secret will reward you in the open.

Based on this scripture, I have a place where I go to be alone with the Lord. There is nothing special about this room, other than I have anointed it as my War Room. I pray, make declarations, seek the face of Jesus, and see into the spirit realm in this room. I encourage you to create a space where you can be uninterrupted for prayer and your secret place with the Lord.

I have had several visions of Jesus in my quiet place. One was very short but oh so life-changing for me. I was worshiping and singing, *I Want to See Jesus*. I was focusing on my spirit, and there He was. He wore a long white robe of the finest yet simple material. His feet were a bronze-like color with brown sandals. His face was wreathed in a smile of love. His eyes were a fiery blue. His hair was long and brown.

When I first saw Him, I had my eyes closed. My eyes popped open, and I quickly shut them, not wanting to lose the vision. Jesus threw His head back and laughed at my expression, then He motioned for me to come toward Him. He then turned and started walking away, still motioning for me to follow. What a special, wonderful moment. I felt like it might have gone further, but I was very emotional and overwhelmed by the glory of seeing Jesus.

For days afterward, I asked Him to show me where He wanted me to follow Him. Then during my morning prayer time, I ask Jesus to meet with me, just the two of us. He appeared to me sitting on a hill. He patted the ground beside Him and motioned for me to sit down. I did and looked over the tree-covered hills, meadows, and stream before us. It was a beautiful place, like a huge garden. I asked Him what I could do for Him today.

He said, "Rest. Today is a day of rest."

I was flooded with love and peace, so happy to be with Him in this precious moment. I was so grateful for this honor of His presence. I know this is where He was leading me in the prior vision. He was leading me to the garden of rest. He knew without me asking that I needed to rest, renew my strength, and refresh my spirit. We looked over the beautiful scene before us, just being together, with no words. Yet all the comfort, joy, and love flowed through me as I sat in His presence.

When the vision ended, I was shaking, crying tears of joy. I really can't explain how precious this time with Jesus was!

I was reminded of that old hymn, *In The Garden*:

I come to the garden alone
While the dew is still on the roses
And the voice I hear, falling on my ear
The Son of God discloses
And He walks with me
And He talks with me
And He tells me I am His own
And the joy we share as tarry there
None other has ever Know
I'd stay in the garden with Him
Though the night around me be falling
But He bids me go
With a voice of woe
His voice to me is calling (written by: Austin Miles)

Mr. Miles must have had a garden experience to have written such a beautiful hymn.

These times with the Lord have been life changing. I want more of Jesus and to spend more time in His presence.

I am in my War Room recording this experience for you, my friend, seek Him, pursue Him, hunger and thirst for Him. If He visits me, He will visit you!

Isaiah 55:6 (Amplified)

6. See, inquire for, and require the Lord while He may be found (claiming Him by necessity and by right). Call upon Him while He is near.

The Bible tells us to seek Him, find Him. If it were not possible, scripture would not have led us to do so. He desires that we pursue Him to have that personal relationship of giving and receiving as you fellowship. A relationship is give and take. The Lord certainly gives more that He takes. He desires your worship, adoration, reverence, and meeting with Him in that secret place of the spirit. So long, we have settled for praying and leaving our petitions with the Lord, church on Sunday, sermon, then Bible study mid-week. It takes more to pursue. Seek and put Him first.

I Corinthians 2:9-13 (Amplified)

9. But on the contrary, as the scripture says, what eye has not seen and ear has not heard and has not entered into the heart of man, (all that) God has prepared (made and keeps ready) for those who love Him (who hold Him in affectionate reverence, promptly obeying Him and gratefully recognizing the benefits He has bestowed).

10. Yet to us, God has unveiled and revealed them by and through His Spirit, for the (Holy) Spirit searches diligently, exploring and examining everything, even sounding the profound and bottomless things of God (the divine counsels and things hidden beyond man's scrutiny),

11. For what person perceives (knows, or understands what passes through a man's thoughts except for the man's own spirit within him? Just so no one discerns (come to know and comprehend) the thoughts of God except the Spirit of God.

12. Now we have not received the spirit (that belongs to), of the world but the (Holy) Spirit who is from God, (given to us) that we realize and comprehend and appreciate the gifts (of divine favor and blessing freely and lavishly) bestowed on us by God.

13. And we are setting these truths forth in words not taught by human wisdom, but taught by the (Holy) Spirit combining and interpreting spiritual truths with spiritual language (to those who possess the (Holy) Spirit.

There are wonderful, exciting, beautiful experiences waiting in the realm of the Holy Spirit. Things we cannot even imagine with our human logic. They are only discerned through the Holy Spirit of God. They are for this present time. Seeing into the spirit realm to access what the Heavenly Father wants to reveal to us through His Son Jesus Christ.

How exciting is that? To know that access is ours through the Holy Spirit. Earlier in this book, I shared the gifts of the Holy Spirit. All those gifts are through `and by the Holy Spirit. The same Spirit that knows the mind of God.

In this chapter, I want you to realize that the Heavenly Father (God), Jesus Christ, and Holy Spirit are the three in one. They work together with our spirits to reveal the deep things of God as we seek, hunger, and pursue the Lord. Ask Jesus to open your spiritual eyes, open your spiritual ears, so that you may see the wonderful things the Lord has to show you.

John 14:16-21 (Amplified)

Jesus said to His disciples:

16. I will ask the Father, and He will give you a comforter (counselor, helper, intercessor, advocate, strengthener, and standby) that He may remain with you forever.

17. The Spirit of Truth, Whom the world cannot receive (welcome, take into its heart) because it does not see Him or know Him and recognize Him. But you know and recognize Him, for He lives in you (constantly) and will be in you.

18. I will not leave you as orphans (comfortless, desolate, bereaved, forlorn, helpless). I will come (back) to you.

19. Just a little while now, and the world will not see Me anymore. You will live also.

20. At that time (when that day comes), you will know (for yourselves) that I am in the Father, and you are in Me, I (am) in you.

21. The person who has my commands and keeps them is the one who really loves Me, and whoever (really) loves Me will be loved by my Father, and I (too) will love him and show him (reveal, manifest) Myself to him. I will let myself be clearly seen by him and make Myself real to him.

These verses back up the reality of seeing Jesus and other spiritual wonders and adventures the Lord will reveal to you as you seek, obey, and pursue. Be open to all Jesus has for you. You will experience visions, dreams, impressions, and revelation to guide you through, to encourage you or another person.

In this chapter, we have covered a lot of scripture to reveal that walking and seeing in the Spirit realm. The adventures awaiting you are fathomless and endless. Why? Because God is eternal, there is no end to His great mercy and grace. Open your heart to all His gifts and experience all He has for you. Your life will never be the same.

There are many verses in the Bible and books written about the Spiritual realm. I encourage you to read them. Surround yourself with people who will encourage you to grow in the prophecy and all the gifts.

Now I want to ask you to find a quiet place where there are few distractions and you have privacy. Seek the Lord there and keep seeking Him till you have a breakthrough. Ask Him to open you to all He has for you. It may be helpful to play instrumental worship music softly. And focus on Jesus, meditate on His works and wonders while He walked this earth.

Prayer: I pray for the God of our Lord Jesus Christ, the Father of glory, to open your eyes to the heavenly realm, to see the great and mighty wonders available to every child of God.

Grant them wisdom and revelation into the deep things of God the Father. Reveal to them how loved and treasured each of your children is to You, Lord, as they wait before you shower them with Your presence and honor them with the knowledge of Your Kingdom.

In Jesus' Name,

Amen

To my readers, I hope you have been encouraged, challenged, and provoked to go deeper in your relationship with the Heavenly Father, Jesus, and the Holy Spirit. To seek those things that are above and beyond in your spiritual growth. It has been a joy writing this book. I pray you will keep your hunger and desire to go on till He calls us home.

Bonnie Baldwin Briggs